# TODAY IS MY FAVORITE DAY PRAYER BOOK

## *PRAYING THROUGH DIFFICULT TIMES*

David Towner

Today is My Favorite Day Prayer Book: Praying Through Difficult Times

TIMFD LLC Publishing
15515 Carrillon Estates Blvd
Tampa, FL 33625

TIMFD

TODAY IS MY FAVORITE DAY

All Scripture verses are taken from the New International Version. Colorado Springs, CO: International Bible Society. (1978, 1984)

Cover design by Ela Raveling of Masterpiece Artwork

Printed in the United States of America

ISBN: 13-978-1-7333442-1-0

## *Praying Through Difficult Times*

When I wrote *Today Is My Favorite Day*, I had many requests to write a small prayer book that would help those going through difficult times. Frankly speaking, I wish I had this little book when I was undergoing multiple surgeries due to cancer, as I experienced financial hardship, relational heartache, and the loss of a loved one. It would've been nice to consistently pray with someone who had gone through some of the same things I was going through at the time. I hope I can be your support through this book.

When you feel overwhelmed, down, frustrated, or in need of encouragement, I suggest you pick up this book and read a prayer with me. In each prayer, you'll find in parenthesis the phrase (name the struggle). I purposely wrote it that way so you could personalize the prayer by speaking out your specific challenge.

Each prayer has a corresponding verse that I hope encourages you. The word of God is powerful, so make sure to speak it out loud, you'll be declaring God's great work in your life. Under the verse is space for you to write your thoughts. I suggest you briefly write down what you received from the prayer and corresponding scripture. If you have time, write down one thing you are thankful for, it will encourage you. I've found writing down my thoughts and thanksgivings at the moment has been an invaluable exercise navigating my dirty dishes, difficult seasons, and devastating events. I believe this simple exercise will also help you to enjoy the journey even in difficult times.

In Christ,

David

*Do not be anxious about anything, but in every situation, by prayer and petition, with thanksgiving, present your requests to God. And the peace of God, which transcends all understanding, will guard your hearts and your minds in Christ Jesus.*
Philippians 4:6-7

# *My Shock*

*I came to You in weakness with great fear and trembling.*
1 Corinthians 2:3

Lord, I'm shocked over the news of (name the struggle). I'm crying out to You for help. I don't know what to do with the reality that my life has been altered. I'm fearful for my future. Please protect my body, spirit, and mind. I feel weak and vulnerable right now, and that's why I am coming to You in prayer. I thank You already, for giving me the strength I need to continue this journey. I implore You, my creator, sustainer, and ruler, and I ask for Your intervention. Only You give me the confidence to overcome my fear and frailty and help me to deal with **my shock** of this new normal. Thank You for being with me. I pray this in Jesus name, Amen.

## *-Notes-*

_____
_____
_____
_____
_____
_____
_____
_____
_____
_____

# *My Help*

*I cried out to God for help; I cried out to God to hear me.*
Psalm 77:1

Lord, I don't know what else to do but come to You. I'm in a dark place, (name the struggle) has got a grip on my heart. I'm crying out to You for help. I need Your wisdom as to what steps I need to take next. I need Your direction as I navigate the changes that are beginning to take place in my life. Please protect me from my own negative thoughts. Thank You for listening to my concerns. Thank You in advance for Your intervention in my life. I wait in anticipation for the relief You will bring to my soul. Thank You for being **my help** in this time of trouble. In Jesus name, I pray. Amen.

## *-Notes-*

_____

_____

_____

_____

_____

_____

_____

_____

_____

# *My Calm*

*Be still and know that I am God.*
Psalm 46:10a

Lord, Your word says to be still, but my mind is going one-hundred miles-an-hour in every direction as I deal with (name the struggle). I'm thinking about too many things. Help me to be still before You. I'm trying to process this feeling of powerlessness. I don't want to let the confusion of fear, worry, and doubt ruin my life. I know You are my God. Help me to rely on You. You are Sovereign, and You hold my future in Your hands. Though I don't fully understand why, I trust You are in control of everything, including my life. You are **my calm** in the middle of the chaos. I pray this in Jesus name, Amen.

*-Notes-*

_____

_____

_____

_____

_____

_____

_____

_____

_____

_____

# *My Peace*

*I have told you these things, so that in Me you may have peace. In this world, you will have trouble. But take heart! I have overcome the world.*
John 16:33b

Lord, it's hard to comprehend the impact (<u>name the struggle</u>) has had on my family and me. I see the long road ahead, and it seems daunting. You say I will experience trouble in this world. You were right, and right now, I don't know exactly what to do about it. You say to take heart, but my heart is heavy. Though You say You have overcome the world, I still feel overwhelmed and stressed. Despite my feelings, I trust in the fact You are all-powerful (omnipotent), and You will help me through this rough time. Despite my emotions, I trust You have a plan for my life. I believe You will help me deal with (<u>name the struggle</u>) and bring quietness to my soul. Thank You for being **my peace**. I pray this in Jesus name, Amen.

*-Notes-*

_____

_____

_____

_____

_____

_____

_____

_____

_____

# *My Joy*

*I do believe; help me overcome my unbelief!*
Mark 9:24

Lord, I've struggled at times believing You're with me. The struggle is real, and I'm wondering if You can and will help me. I'm finding it hard to believe in Your ability to overcome (<u>name the struggle</u>). Forgive me for that, but I want to be honest with You. My faith is waning, please help me. I need You. Help me with my unbelief. I know my faith shouldn't run by my emotions. The fact is You're omnipresent, You are always everywhere. That means You are with me right now, and that truth brings a smile to my face. I believe You can do all things, even defeat (name the struggle). Thank You for being the center of my joy. I pray this in Jesus name, Amen.

*-Notes-*

_____
_____
_____
_____
_____
_____
_____
_____
_____
_____

# *My Courage*

*The Lord is near to all who call on Him, to all who call on Him in truth.*
Psalm 145:18

Lord, in my despair, I call out to You. I am dealing with (name the struggle), and I need You now. My feelings are waning, but I trust in the fact You are with me even when my feelings fade. You are omnipresent. You are everywhere, always, and I know You are with me in this dark and challenging time. You told the Israelite people as they were about to enter *The Promised Land*, "I will never leave you nor forsake you." Your words gave them the courage to take the land. The truth is, You never change. You are always the same. Therefore, I know You will never leave me nor forsake me. Your presence is the reason for **my courage**. I pray this in Jesus name, Amen.

*-Notes-*

_____

_____

_____

_____

_____

_____

_____

_____

_____

# *My Assurance*

*I will remember the deeds of the Lord; yes, I will remember Your miracles of long ago. I will consider all Your works and meditate on all Your mighty deeds.*
Psalm 77:11-12

Lord, in my battle with (name the struggle) sometimes I forget what You've done. You created everything. You brought freedom to Your people by releasing ten plagues on Egypt and splitting the Red Sea. You healed the blind, lame, and sick. You gave me life in the here and now and You give me eternal life in heaven. I will meditate on all Your excellent work and look forward to what You are going to do in the future with me. You are **my assurance** for a good today and a blessed tomorrow. I know it doesn't mean everything will be perfect, but I find peace in placing my future in the One who is. I pray this in Jesus name, Amen.

*-Notes-*

_____

_____

_____

_____

_____

_____

_____

_____

_____

# *My Freedom*

*Turn to me and be gracious to me, for I am lonely and afflicted. Relieve the troubles of my heart and free me from my anguish.*
Psalm 25:16-17

Lord, I need You. I'm letting (name the struggle) get the best of me. There are days when I want to whine and complain to everyone. There are other days that I want to isolate. I'm frustrated, and my demeanor has been awful at times. Only You can help me get my mind into a healthier place. Only You can free me from my poor attitude and give me a favorite day mindset. Thank You, in advance, for the gift of today and helping me to take advantage of every moment. Only You can release me from this loneliness, anguish, and affliction. Thank You for **my freedom** that drives me to live each day fully with You. I pray this in Jesus name, Amen.

## *-Notes-*

_____

_____

_____

_____

_____

_____

_____

_____

_____

# *My Serenity*

*Set your minds on things above, not on earthly things.*
Colossians 3:2

Lord, give me a different point of view. Help me to live in the present and focus on the things that really matter. I admit, sometimes I get focused on money, future bills, and material things and I lose track of You. I know those things are essential to deal with, but without You guiding me, they can feel overwhelming. Help me to set my mind on You as I deal with (name the struggle). I want to seek Your peace and wisdom as I navigate my new normal. You are the cause of **my serenity**. Thank You for setting my mind on things above and not get caught up so much into (name the struggle). I pray this in Jesus name, Amen.

*-Notes-*

_____
_____
_____
_____
_____
_____
_____
_____
_____

# *My Comfort*

*Praise be to the God and Father of our Lord Jesus Christ, the Father of compassion and the God of all comfort, who comforts us in all our troubles, so that we can comfort those in any trouble with the comfort we ourselves receive from God.*
2 Corinthians 1:3-4

Lord, I praise You for Your consistent support. Though (name the struggle) has many times occupied my mind, I take solace in knowing You are always by my side. You bring me peace, and You are the source of **my comfort**. You are there for me as I deal with (name the struggle) and I want to be there for others in their times of trouble. Today, I ask You to help me get my attention off my own problems and turn my heart to be ready to uplift others. Thank You, in advance, for the opportunities You're going to give me to comfort others. I pray this in Jesus name, Amen.

*-Notes-*

_____
_____
_____
_____
_____
_____
_____
_____
_____
_____

## *My Provider*

*Therefore, I tell you, do not worry about your life, what you will eat or drink; or about your body, what you will wear. Is not life more than food, and the body more than clothes? Look at the birds of the air; they do not sow or reap or store away in barns, and yet your heavenly Father feeds them. Are you not much more valuable than they?*
Matthew 6:25-26

Lord, I do worry about my future. I get anxious wondering if (name the struggle) will permanently change my life. I fear that it will get worse. I struggle with the unknown. You tell me not to worry about my future. But I do worry. You say if You take care of the birds of the air, You will certainly take care of me. But I question Your attention to me as I fight (name the struggle). You declare I am valuable to You, but I struggle to believe it. You express to me not to worry about material things, but I do. Help me to accept the truth that I matter to You, and You have a plan to take care of me. Thank You for being **my provider**. I pray this in Jesus name, Amen.

*-Notes-*

_____

_____

_____

_____

_____

_____

_____

_____

_____

_____

# *My Solace*

*Can any one of you by worrying add a single hour to your life?*
Matthew 6:27

Lord, I admit it, I worry sometimes. I worry about my future, my family, my finances, and my outcome as I deal with (name the struggle). You say that worrying won't add an hour to my life, so why do I do it? Why am I trying to do things in my own power? Forgive me for getting caught up in what I can't do and help me to get focused on all You can do. You are all-powerful (omnipotent). You are all-knowing (omniscient). You are always present (omnipresent). I place my worries into Your infinite hands. You are **my solace**. Thank You for taking my anxiety and doubt from me. I pray this in Jesus name, Amen.

## *-Notes-*

_____

_____

_____

_____

_____

_____

_____

_____

# *My Relief*

*Cast all your anxiety on Him because He cares for you.*
1 Peter 5:7

Lord, I'm anxious about my future as I struggle with (name your struggle). Help me to live each minute, hour, and day with You. Keep me from drifting away from You. There are moments that I have tried to deal with this on my own. I confess I can't. I'm casting all my pain, worry, and doubt on You. I acknowledge you are God, and I am not. I can't keep on trying to carry the weight of (name your struggle) in my own power. Thank You for gladly taking my anxieties from me. Thank You for loving and caring for me. Your presence is the reason for **my relief**. I pray this in Jesus name, Amen.

*-Notes-*

_____
_____
_____
_____
_____
_____
_____
_____
_____
_____

# *My Patience*

*I waited patiently for the Lord; He turned to me and heard my cry.*
Psalm 40:1

Lord, I am reaching out to You in desperation. Thank You for listening to my pleas for help. I'm concerned about my future as I face (name the struggle). I'm waiting patiently for you to answer my prayers. Though I'm small and insignificant compared to the rest of this world, I know You hear my cries for help. It's because of Your greatness that **my patience** grows, waiting in anticipation of your miraculous work. This I know, You are turning towards me and intently listening to me. This I know, I matter to You, You love me, and You care for me. And this I know, You are working in my life. Thank You. I pray this in Jesus name, Amen.

*-Notes-*

_____

_____

_____

_____

_____

_____

_____

_____

_____

# *My Clarity*

*But seek first His kingdom and His righteousness, and all these things will be given to you as well.*
Matthew 6:33

Lord, help me to seek You with every fiber of my body. Help me to be cognizant of each breath You give me. Though I am dealing with (name the struggle) I am not defined by it. Help me to enjoy each moment with You. I desire to connect with You in ways I've never experienced before. Even with the uneasiness and uncertainty of my future, my desire for You grows. You are **my clarity**. You gave Your life for me. You rose from the dead to show Your power over death. You have given me an eternal future in heaven. I clearly see Your love for me. Thank You. I pray this in Jesus name, Amen.

*-Notes-*

_____
_____
_____
_____
_____
_____
_____
_____
_____
_____

# *My Margin*

*Therefore, do not worry about tomorrow, for tomorrow will worry about itself. Each day has enough trouble of its own.*
Matthew 6:34

Lord, it's so easy to get caught up in my (name the struggle) and worry about my future. I've let myself get worked up about the things that may happen tomorrow and lose focus on what's happening right now. Help me to be present. I may not know what tomorrow holds, but I know You want me to enjoy today. I place my tomorrows into Your perfect control. You hold my future. You chose to give me this day, so help me to make the most out of it. Help me to love, laugh, learn, and listen well with all those I come in contact today. Knowing I don't have to worry about tomorrow is liberating. You are **my margin** so I can enjoy today. I pray this in Jesus name, Amen.

## *-Notes-*

_____

_____

_____

_____

_____

_____

_____

_____

_____

# *My Rest*

*Come to Me, all you who are weary and burdened, and I will give you rest.*
Matthew 11:28

Lord, I'm feeling overloaded. The impact (name the struggle) is having on my life is overwhelming at times. I feel tired, worn-out, even to the point of exhaustion. The weight of all that is going on around me is pushing me to my limit. I can't seem to find rest, so I come to You for help. You say You will give me rest. I don't know how, but I believe You will slow down my mind so I can find calmness. I trust You will relax my body so I can sleep. I know you are the creator and provider of peacefulness, so I will lean on You to grant it to me. You are **my rest**. I pray this in Jesus name, Amen.

*-Notes-*

_____
_____
_____
_____
_____
_____
_____
_____
_____
_____

# *My Tranquility*

*Take My yoke upon you and learn from Me, for I am gentle and humble in heart, and you will find rest for your souls. For My yoke is easy, and My burden is light.*
Matthew 11:29-30

Lord, You challenge me to lean and rely on You, and as I do, I will find rest. Rest is appealing as I deal with (name the struggle). I'm stressed and tired, and it seems impossible to relax. Guide me to see Your perfect rest for my weary mind, body, and soul. It's scary to take Your yoke and release full control over to You, but I need to. This (name the struggle) is too much for me to bear. I need Your help. My heart's desire is to find rest and comfort in You. You are **my tranquility**. Just thinking about releasing control puts me in a peaceful frame of mind. Thank You. I pray this in Jesus name, Amen.

## *-Notes-*

_____
_____
_____
_____
_____
_____
_____
_____
_____
_____

# *My Shelter*

*The Lord is good, a refuge in times of trouble. He cares for those who trust in Him.*
Nahum 1:7

Lord, I don't know what the future holds but I entrust my today and my tomorrows to You. I know You love and genuinely care about me. As I deal with (name the struggle) I will take refuge in You. When I feel weak, I will rely on Your strength (omnipotent). When I'm undecided, I will depend on Your wisdom. When I don't know the answers, I will seek Your knowledge (omniscient). When I'm in trouble and fearful, I will count on Your guidance. You are good, and I know You will help me navigate my next steps. You are **my shelter,** and You bring harmony to my life. I pray this in Jesus name, Amen.

*-Notes-*

_____
_____
_____
_____
_____
_____
_____
_____
_____
_____

# *My Motivation*

*The Lord Himself goes before you and will be with you; He will never leave you nor forsake you. Do not be afraid; do not be discouraged.*
Deuteronomy 31:8

Lord, I don't know what tomorrow will bring, but you promise You will be with me as I deal with the devastating effects of (name the struggle). It's hard to fathom that You, infinite God, would give me the time of day, but You do. You say You will not leave me as I go through my trying times. It's tough to believe that the creator and sustainer of all life would care about me that much, but You do. Because You are with me, I will not fear (name the struggle), and I will not let it discourage me. You are **my motivation** to live courageously despite the difficulties. Thank You for being present in my life. I pray this in Jesus name, Amen.

## *-Notes-*

_____
_____
_____
_____
_____
_____
_____
_____
_____

# *My Optimism*

*And my God will meet all your needs according to the riches of His glory in Christ Jesus.*
Philippians 4:19

Lord, I need Your help as I deal with (name the struggle). I need You to meet my physical needs. There are days when I'm exhausted, and I wonder if I have the fight to carry on. I need You to meet my emotional needs. Sometimes I feel I have nothing else to give to my family and friends. I need You to meet my spiritual needs. There are moments when I feel disconnected to You. Help me, even when I feel run down to seek the truth in Your word. I don't know how you will meet my needs, but Your Scripture tells me to joyfully trust You. You are the reason for **my optimism,** and I thank You for whatever You will do in the future. I pray this in Jesus name, Amen.

*-Notes-*

_____
_____
_____
_____
_____
_____
_____
_____
_____
_____
_____

# My Faithfulness

*For we live by faith, not by sight.*
2 Corinthians 5:7

Lord, living by faith is sometimes painful. There are days when I can't see You working, and I want to take control of my (name the struggle). Placing my life entirely in Your hands, I know is best, but there are days when it's so difficult to do. Help me to trust you completely. Strengthen my weak faith so I can confidently say, "I live by faith and not by sight." I look forward to seeing the great things You have in store for my life. You created the universe and split the Red Sea. You walked on water and healed the sick. You have proven to be trustworthy. You are the inspiration to **my faithfulness**. I pray this in Jesus name, Amen.

*-Notes-*

_____

_____

_____

_____

_____

_____

_____

_____

# *My Patience*

*Wait for the Lord; be strong and take heart and wait for the Lord.*
Psalm 27:14

Lord, one of the toughest things to do for me is to wait. Patience may be a virtue, but right now, I just don't see the value in it. I want to trust You as I deal with (name the struggle), but sometimes I just want to see some positive progress. I understand Your timing is not my timing. Help me to rely on You during this waiting time and not try to push my own agenda and time table. I know You have my best interests at heart. During this time, teach me more about Your character and open my mind to learn and apply it in my daily life. You drive me to become better. You are at the epicenter of **my patience**. Without You, my impatience would overwhelm me and bring me down. Thank you. I pray this in Jesus name, Amen.

### *-Notes-*

_____
_____
_____
_____
_____
_____
_____
_____
_____
_____

# *My Protector*

*Guard my life and rescue me; do not let me be put to shame, for I take refuge in You.*
Psalm 25:20

Lord, rescue me from physical, emotional, and spiritual attacks that come from (name the struggle). Keep my heart from fear. Protect my mind from worry, anxiety, and doubt. Whenever I want to run away from You draw me closer. Every time I want to reach out to something else other than You to ease the pain guide me to You. Help me not to look for anything or anyone that may give temporary gratification and move me further from You. Give me the wisdom to take refuge in You even in the challenging and devastating times. Guard every aspect of my life. You are **my protector**. You make me feel safe. I pray this in Jesus name, Amen.

## *-Notes-*

_____
_____
_____
_____
_____
_____
_____
_____
_____
_____

# *My Deliverer*

*I sought the Lord, and He answered me; He delivered me from all my fears.*
Psalm 34:4

Lord, there are days where fear gets a grip on my emotions. I let (name the struggle) dominate my thinking, which drives me to dread my future. When those days come, I will draw near to You. When I'm anxious, help me to stay on Your firm foundation. When I'm apprehensive, move me to take my next step of faith. When I'm fearful, inspire me to be a courageous follower of You. Guide me away from those things that cause me to fear and toward You who will deliver me from ALL my fears. I stand on the truth that You are **my deliverer**. You make me brave. I pray this in Jesus name, Amen.

*-Notes-*

_____
_____
_____
_____
_____
_____
_____
_____
_____

# *My Sanctuary*

*Peace I leave with you; My peace I give you. I do not give to you as the world gives. Do not let your hearts be troubled and do not be afraid.*
John 14:27

Lord, I will trust You to help me overcome my fears as I deal with (name the struggle). I will depend on You when my troubles seem overwhelming. You say, "Do not be afraid," and so, right now, I commit my life, my will, my fears, and my doubts to Your care and control. I don't want to continue to feel stressed and anxious because I know they are not healthy emotions. I choose to think differently today. I will rely on You for the peace that surpasses all understanding. I've decided to count on You, the Prince of Peace, to give me rest for my soul. You are **my sanctuary**. I pray this in Jesus name, Amen.

*-Notes-*

_____
_____
_____
_____
_____
_____
_____
_____
_____

# *My Encouragement*

*But Jesus immediately said to them: "Take courage! It is I. Don't be afraid."*
Matthew 14:27

Lord, thank you for encouraging me when I'm down. I don't want (name your struggle) to control my thinking or my attitude. Thank You for commanding me to take courage. I know You don't want me to live in timidity. Thank You for telling me to not be afraid. I choose to live confidently in You because of all the incredible things You have done. You made the lame walk. You healed the sick. You brought sight to the blind. You made the mute to talk. You brought people back from the dead. I trust You will help me to take courage as I deal with (name the struggle). Your mighty acts are **my encouragement**. I pray this in Jesus name, Amen.

## *-Notes-*

_____
_____
_____
_____
_____
_____
_____
_____
_____
_____

27

# *My Stability*

*So do not fear, for I am with you; do not be dismayed, for I am your God.*
Isaiah 41:10a

Lord, I trust You are with me as I deal with (name the struggle). I'm not alone. Though I may feel lonely at times, You are there. In my darkest times, You are there. You will never leave me or forsake me. Though (name the struggle) sometimes feels impossible to deal with You are my source of strength. I find peace in knowing You are the God of the impossible. When I get discouraged, You are there to lift me up and give me courage. I will not fear (name the struggle) for you are my God, and there is no one like You. You are **my stability** during this difficult time. I pray this in Jesus name, Amen.

*-Notes-*

_____
_____
_____
_____
_____
_____
_____
_____
_____

# *My Delight*

*When anxiety was great within me, Your consolation brought me joy.*
Psalm 94:19

Lord, I admit I have been anxious. It's tough to be at peace when I have (name the struggle) looming over my life. I confess I haven't been joyful. It's hard to be joyful when my future seems bleak. I acknowledge I've let fear control my thoughts. It's difficult to be courageous when this pain continuously consumes me. Despite all this, I thank You for being with me every step of the way. When I feel low, I look to You, the maker of all joy, to lift me up. My happiness is not dictated by (name the struggle), on the contrary, **my delight** is made complete in Your unfailing love for me. Thank You for making me feel treasured. I pray this in Jesus name, Amen.

*-Notes-*

_____
_____
_____
_____
_____
_____
_____
_____
_____
_____

# My Hope

*Show me Your ways, Lord, teach me Your paths. Guide me in Your*
*truth and teach me, for You are God my Savior, and my hope is in*
*You all day long.*
Psalm 25:4-5

Lord, I don't want to stop living as I deal with (name the struggle). It's so easy to isolate myself when confronted with a life-altering event. Instead of detaching, I choose to engage with You. Show me how I can live a full life today. Help me to apply your word in my life. Teach me how to love well, forgive more, and to listen better. Guide me to be present. Move me to follow Your word. Move me to live in your truth. Thank You for keeping me from a life of seclusion and loneliness. You are **my hope**! Thank You being my Savior now and for eternity. I pray this in Jesus name, Amen.

*-Notes-*

_____
_____
_____
_____
_____
_____
_____
_____
_____
_____

# *My Recovery*

*But He was pierced for our transgressions, He was crushed for our iniquities; the punishment that brought us peace was on Him, and by His wounds we are healed.*
Isaiah 53:5

Lord, You are my great healer. If You choose, You can overcome (name the struggle). I pray for Your hand on my life that I may be fully restored. I also know You heal my eternal soul. You gave Your life so I may live fully here on earth and live supremely happy forever in heaven. Through your sacrifice, I experience the peace that surpasses my limited understanding. Even as I deal with (name the struggle) I know the wounds You endured from the scourging, and the cross was eternally intended to bring healing to me. Thank You for my eternal healing and being the catalyst for **my recovery**. I pray this in Jesus name, Amen.

*-Notes-*

_____
_____
_____
_____
_____
_____
_____
_____
_____
_____

# *My Defense*

*I will say of the LORD, "He is my refuge and my fortress, my God, in whom I trust."*
Psalm 91:2

Lord, I don't know what tomorrow will bring. I don't know if I will overcome (name the struggle). You oversee the creation, including me. I do understand, You know every hair on my head and every cell in my body. I do know I can take refuge in You while stressing over my dirty dishes, struggling with my difficult seasons, and working through my devastating events. Though I'm rattled at times by (name the struggle), I will trust You. You are **my defense**, protecting every cell in my body, every relationship in my life, and every thought in mind. I pray this in Jesus name, Amen.

## *-Notes-*

_____

_____

_____

_____

_____

_____

_____

_____

_____

# *My Victory*

*But thanks be to God! He gives us the victory through our Lord Jesus Christ.*
1 Corinthians 15:57

Lord, today I want to thank You. Thank you for letting me breathe today. Thank You for being with me as I deal with (name the struggle). Thank You for loving me when I feel unlovable. Thank You for giving me direction to my sometimes-chaotic life. Thank You for giving me the purpose to love You and love the people of this world better every day. Thank You for my eternal future in heaven with You. Thank You for making each day, my favorite. Thank You for opening my mind to the possibility of living each moment fully and joyfully. No matter what tomorrow brings, I thank You already for giving me the precious gift of a victorious life. You are **my victory**. I pray this in Jesus name, Amen.

## *-Notes-*

_____
_____
_____
_____
_____
_____
_____
_____
_____
_____

# *My Inspiration*

*He put a new song in my mouth, a hymn of praise to our God. Many will see and fear the Lord and put their trust in Him.*
Psalm 40:3

Lord, thank You for giving me a joyful life despite (name the struggle). As I learn to live in my new normal You have given me a new perspective; one of love, courage, and hope. I will not fear my future because I've put my trust in You; my creator, sustainer, and ruler. You have placed a new song in my mouth; a song of praise to my all-powerful, all-knowing, ever-present God. Thank You for being **my inspiration**. You help me endure (name the struggle) with delight in my heart. Please use me to share Your love with those in my life so they may see Your continual work in me. I pray this in Jesus name, Amen.

*-Notes-*

_____
_____
_____
_____
_____
_____
_____
_____
_____

# *My Direction*

*I will strengthen you and help you; I will uphold you with My righteous right hand.*
Isaiah 41:10b

Lord, You are perfect and righteous, and I am not. Therefore, I release my need for control, and I give my future and (name the struggle) into Your flawless and all-powerful hands. I stand on Your promise to give me strength when I'm weak. I lean on Your commitment to helping me in my best times and when I'm at my worst. I praise You for upholding me when I feel I have nowhere to go and nothing else to give. You are God, and I am not, and I'm okay with that. Remind me to always rely on You. Help me to be sensitive to Your leading and gently guide me when I move from Your path. You are **my direction**. I pray this in Jesus name, Amen.

*-Notes-*

_____
_____
_____
_____
_____
_____
_____
_____
_____
_____

# *My Strength*

*He gives strength to the weary and increases the power of the weak.*
Isaiah 40:29

Lord, I need Your strength and power today. I'm exhausted. The continual stress from dealing with (name the struggle) is wearing me out. There are days when I don't perceive Your presence, but the truth is, You're with me. There are moments when I don't sense Your love, but the fact is, You do love me. There are times when I don't feel Your help, but Your word says, You're guiding and sometimes carrying me on this journey. Thank You for being **my strength**, not only to survive but thrive today. I pray this in Jesus name, Amen.

## *-Notes-*

_____
_____
_____
_____
_____
_____
_____
_____
_____
_____

# *My Reason*

*Be joyful in hope, patient in affliction, faithful in prayer.*
Romans 12:12

Lord, thank You for being the reason for my joy. It's hard sometimes to be joyful when I am continually dealing with (name the struggle). But when I look to You, I know I have a hopeful future. Right now, I rejoice in the truths that You are with me and love me today, tomorrow, and forever. Even when my life gets complicated, You give me the patience to endure for I know my eternal destiny is with You in heaven. Thank You for listening to my prayers. Help me to faithfully listen to You more. You are **my reason** for being joyful despite (name the struggle). I pray this in Jesus name, Amen.

*-Notes-*

_____
_____
_____
_____
_____
_____
_____
_____
_____

# *My Rescuer*

*He lifted me out of the slimy pit, out of the mud and mire; He set my feet on a rock and gave me a firm place to stand.*
Psalm 40:2

Lord, thank You for reaching out to me in my darkness, painfulness, and devastation. I'm reaching out to You in this dim time. I have let (name the struggle) take me down an ugly path in my mind. I have not been the best example of faithfulness, so I'm relying on Your commitment to me. You gave Your life on the cross so I may live forever with You in heaven. You forgave my sins of anger, fear, resentment, and bitterness so I may learn to love You and others better every day. Thank you for being **my rescuer** and pulling me out of the depths of despair to give me a life of love now and forever. I pray this in Jesus name, Amen.

## *-Notes-*

_____

_____

_____

_____

_____

_____

_____

_____

_____

## *My Sustainer*

*Cast your cares on the Lord, and He will sustain you; He will never let the righteous be shaken.*
Psalm 55:22

Lord, today I place my cares that stem from (name the struggle) in Your all-powerful (omnipotent) hands. I've been trying to control everything in my power, and I know it is unsustainable. I can't continue to be my own (little g) god; I don't have the capacity. But You say if I give my worries entirely to You, then I won't be shaken. If I receive positive or negative news about (name the struggle), I trust You will take care of it. You are **my sustainer.** No matter what goes on in my life, I will look to You to help me endure. I pray this in Jesus name, Amen.

*-Notes-*

_____

_____

_____

_____

_____

_____

_____

_____

_____

_____

# *My Love*

*Let them give thanks to the Lord for His unfailing love and His wonderful deeds for mankind.*
Psalm 107:21

Lord, You passionately loved me before I even thought about loving You. You love me even when I'm dealing with (name the struggle). Your love is constant. Your love is always there encouraging me to continue. Your love is merciful. Thank You for not giving me what I deserve. Your love is forgiving. Though I've been unfaithful at times, You still pour out Your love to me. Your love is gracious. Though I don't deserve Your love, You give it freely. You showed Your unfailing love for me through the beatings, crucifixion, burial, and wonderous resurrection. Because You loved me first, you are my first love today. Help me to learn to love those in my life as You love me. I declare You are **my passion**. I pray this in Jesus name, Amen.

*-Notes-*

_____
_____
_____
_____
_____
_____
_____
_____
_____
_____

# *My Perspective*

*Not only so, but we also glory in our sufferings, because we know that suffering produces perseverance; perseverance, character; and character, hope.*
Romans 5:3-4

Lord, I didn't ask for and never wanted to deal with (name the struggle). No one wants to suffer and experience troubles in life. But now that I'm facing it, I ask You to help me with **my perspective**. It would easy to give up, to call it quits, and fall apart but I know You don't want that for me. Help me to learn from this challenging chapter in my life. Teach me to persevere through the pain and worry. Guide me to develop Your loving and joyful character. Let me see the hope I have with You, now and for eternity. Grow in me a passion to live fully. I pray this in Jesus name, Amen.

*-Notes-*

_____
_____
_____
_____
_____
_____
_____
_____
_____
_____
_____

## *My Gaze*

*They will have no fear of bad news; their hearts are steadfast, trusting
in the Lord.*
Psalm 112:7

Lord, I declare my dependence on You as I deal with (name the struggle). I will not fear this bad news or any other devastating news for I will steadfastly keep my eyes on You. As I gaze at Your glory, the problems seem smaller. As I look at Your power, the struggles don't seem so insurmountable. As I stare at Your wisdom and knowledge, the complications don't seem so difficult. I will gaze at Your character, your love, and your truth, and I will glance at the problems I'm facing with (name the struggle). **My gaze** will remain steadfastly on You, my creator, and healer. I pray this in Jesus name, Amen.

## *-Notes-*

_____

_____

_____

_____

_____

_____

_____

_____

_____

# *My Sleep*

*In peace I will lie down and sleep, for You alone, Lord, make me dwell in safety.*
Psalm 4:8

Lord, many times, I have struggled to sleep. I admit I've let (name the struggle) rob me of my rest. I confess I have worried over the prospects of my future. But today, I place **my sleep** and my rest in Your hands. I don't want to stress over what may happen. I don't want to be anxious about what could be. I don't want to be nervous about what may come next. I want to live in the present with You. I want to live in a peaceful state that is centered on Your love and care for me. So today, I will rest safely in You. I choose to give You **my sleep** knowing You are in control. I pray this in Jesus name, Amen.

*-Notes-*

# *My Determination*

*I will instruct you and teach you in the way you should go; I will counsel you with My loving eye on you.*
Psalm 32:8

Lord, as I deal with (name the struggle) I'm finding joy knowing You will instruct me through it all. As I go into this battle, I'm finding victory, not in my strength but in Your infinite power. As I enter this new normal, I'm building confidence knowing You will teach me Your wise and beautiful ways. As I walk through this dark valley, I'm experiencing peace for my weary heart knowing You are watching over me. As I step into this vast unknown, I'm developing courage because You have my future in Your hands. You are the impetus of **my determination** to overcome anything that comes my way. Thank you for Your presence in my life. I pray this in Jesus name, Amen.

*-Notes-*

# *My Shield*

*Every word of God is flawless; He is a shield to those who take refuge in Him.*
Proverbs 30:5

Lord, I will rely on Your unchanging and unfathomable perfect word. Your word will help keep my mind from being consumed by the news of (name your struggle). Your word promises healing to my body. In it, I find rest for my soul. In it, I see hope for my future. Your Scripture tells me I will experience peace in my heart. In it, I experience joy in my being. In it, I experience hope for my future. Your word is **my shield** against worry and doubt. Your word is my refuge that guards me against the stresses of (name the struggle). Thank You for Your word. I pray this in Jesus name, Amen.

## *-Notes-*

_____
_____
_____
_____
_____
_____
_____
_____
_____
_____

# My Patience

*I waited patiently for the Lord; He turned to me and heard my cry.*
Psalm 40:1

Lord, I am reaching out to You in desperation. Thank You for listening to my pleas for help. I'm concerned about my future as I face (name the struggle). I'm waiting patiently for You to answer my prayers. Though I'm small and insignificant compared to the rest of this world, I know You hear my cries for help. It's because of Your greatness that **my patience** grows, waiting in anticipation of your miraculous work. This I know, You are turning towards me and intently listening to me. This I know, I matter to You, You love me, and You care for me. And this I know, You are working in my life. Thank You. I pray this in Jesus name, Amen.

*-Notes-*

_____

_____

_____

_____

_____

_____

_____

_____

_____

# *My Happiness*

*Anxiety weighs down the heart, but a kind word cheers it up.*
Proverbs 12:25

Lord, You are the reason for **my happiness**. Even (name the struggle) can't take Your joy from me. Help to overcome my negative self-talk by speaking of the greatness of You. Lead me to defeat my anxiety and angst with the truth of Your word. Change my heart to speak kind, positive, and uplifting words. I declare, "Today is my favorite day" with a smile on my face knowing no matter what comes my way, You are there cheering me on. I will praise Your name with laughter knowing that many times You will pick me up and carry me through those dark times. Thank You for changing my attitude from desolation and despair to happiness and contentment. I pray this in Jesus name, Amen.

*-Notes-*

_____
_____
_____
_____
_____
_____
_____
_____
_____
_____

# *My Weakness*

*Finally, be strong in the Lord and in His mighty power.*
Ephesians 6:10

Lord, You are all-powerful (omnipotent). There is nothing, and there is no one who compares to You. You are the originator of everything that has ever been and will ever be. You're so powerful that You calmed the seas, healed the masses, and fed thousands with five loaves and two fish. That's why I'm coming to You for help. I need Your strength to endure (name the struggle). I know in **my weakness**, I am strong because of You. I can overcome anything that comes my way. Thank You for making me secure in You and in Your mighty power. I pray this in Jesus name, Amen.

*-Notes-*

_____
_____
_____
_____
_____
_____
_____
_____
_____
_____

# *My Resolution*

*For the Spirit God gave us does not make us timid, but gives us power,*
*love, and self-discipline.*
*2 Timothy 1:7*

Lord, thank You for Your Spirit living in me. You make me courageous. This is **my resolution**, I will not fear (name the struggle). I resolve not to live in timidity but to live boldly knowing You give me the power to defeat anything this world wants to throw at me. You've shown Your powerful love through Your sacrifice on the cross. I resolve to love the people in my life with Your passion; sacrificially, selflessly, and with a servants heart. I'm deciding to rely on Your power, to live a disciplined life, and not fall into the traps of isolation, bitterness, anger, or fear. This is my resolution. I pray this in Jesus name, Amen.

*-Notes-*

# *My Mourning*

*Blessed are those who mourn, for they will be comforted.*
Matthew 5:4

Lord, help me to mourn well. It sounds odd, but I'm struggling with my emotions, and I need Your guidance. (Name the struggle) has caused pain and unwanted changes. There are days when I get angry because my life has been severely altered. Help me to grieve my previous life, and accept my new normal. I ask You to guide me through this process so I may find healing. Thank You for Your promised comfort as I work through **my mourning**. Let me fully embrace and enjoy Your heavenly comfort so, one day in the future, I may show Your compassion to someone in need. I pray this in Jesus name, Amen.

*-Notes-*

_____
_____
_____
_____
_____
_____
_____
_____
_____

# *My God*

*But I trust in You, LORD; I say, "You are my God."*
Psalm 31:14

Lord, You are my God, and I will praise Your holy name. There is nothing You can't do. You promised Abraham a mighty nation. You promised land to the people of Israel. You promised a virgin birth. You are beyond reliable, all Your promises come true. I place my trust, my life, and my future in Your mighty hands. You choose to give me life. You elect to be with me through my (name the struggle). You love me when I feel unlovable. You encourage me when I'm stressed out and irritable. Thank You for being **my God,** who has decided to give me eternal life. I pray this in Jesus name, Amen.

*-Notes-*

_____
_____
_____
_____
_____
_____
_____
_____
_____
_____
_____

# *My Savior*

*The LORD is close to the brokenhearted and saves those who are crushed in spirit.*
Psalm 34:18

Lord, forgive me, I've tried to take control of my (name the struggle) in my power, and it isn't working. It's crushing, and the stress is too high. I admit I have a control problem, I'm a CFF (Control Freak Friend). I keep making plans without You, and all it's brought me is a crushed spirit. I've tried to be independent, believing I I don't need Your help, but I was wrong. I'm broken, but I rejoice in knowing You're close to me even when I'm smug. I confess I need Your help. You are my Savior. Thank You for redeeming me from my foolishness, arrogance, and pride. I look in anticipation of the great things You're going to do in my life. I pray this in Jesus name, Amen.

## *-Notes-*

_____

_____

_____

_____

_____

_____

_____

_____

_____

_____

# *My Shepherd*

*Even though I walk through the darkest valley, I will fear no evil, for*
*You are with me; Yyour rod and Your staff, they comfort me.*
Psalm 23:4

Lord, it feels like I've been walking in a dark valley for some time now. It's been on a rough road dealing with (name the struggle). I know I live in a fallen world and things like (name the struggle) are a part of it. Though I feel down, I am not out, and I will not live in fear. You are always with me (omnipresent). You'll protect me just like a shepherd would protect His sheep. You'll stave off the enemy and keep me from falling into his traps of worry, doubt, anger, and fear. Your presence gives me comfort because the God of the universe knows my name and fights for me. Thank You for being **my shepherd**. I pray this in Jesus name, Amen.

*-Notes-*

_____
_____
_____
_____
_____
_____
_____
_____
_____

# *My Awakening*

*But those who hope in the Lord will renew their strength. They will soar on wings like eagles; they will run and not grow weary, they will walk and not be faint.*
Isaiah 40:31

Lord, before (name the struggle) I lived in strength, endurance, and self-assurance. I didn't think much of You. I lived on my terms, at least, that's what I thought. But lately, I've been living in weakness, weariness, and worry. So, now, I humbly come to You for help. I once placed my hope in me. I now know how foolish that was, and today I put my hope entirely in You. Awaken my soul and lead me. Speak to me, and I will listen. I believe You will renew my strength. I trust I will soar in Your love. I have faith I will endure in Your hope. Thank You for being **my awakening** and restoring my life. I pray this in Jesus name, Amen.

## *-Notes-*

_____
_____
_____
_____
_____
_____
_____
_____
_____
_____

# *My Maker*

*I lift up my eyes to the mountains—where does my help come from? My help comes from the LORD, the Maker of heaven, and earth.*
Psalm 121:1-2

Lord, I look to the skies, and I see Your creativity. I look at the mountains, and I observe Your vastness. I gaze at the seas and grasp Your splendor. You are the maker and sustainer of heaven and earth, and my help comes from You and no one else. As I fight (name the struggle), I'm at peace knowing You are **my maker**. You created every cell in my body. I know You'll protect and heal me. You know every thought in my mind. Grant me wisdom to make the right decisions. You know the plans You have for me. Guide and lead me to follow You on this journey. Thank You for Your incredible help, my maker, creator, and sustainer. I pray this in Jesus name, Amen.

*-Notes-*

_____

_____

_____

_____

_____

_____

_____

_____

_____

# *My Restoration*

*And the God of all grace, who called you to His eternal glory in Christ, after you have suffered a little while, will Himself restore you and make you strong, firm and steadfast.*
1 Peter 5:10

Lord, I know in this world we will suffer. This is an imperfect place filled with pain, hurt, disappointment, and (name the struggle). I'm anguishing now, but I know my restoration will come. I also know this is not my permanent home. You have an eternal place ready for me in heaven. I acknowledge I receive this forever gift through your magnificent grace. In the meantime, I'm dealing with the difficulties of this world right now, and I'm searching for the strength and steadfastness that only comes from You. Restore my brokenness and make whole. Thank You for **my restoration** now and in eternity. I pray this in Jesus name, Amen.

## *-Notes-*

_____

_____

_____

_____

_____

_____

_____

_____

_____

# *My Cry*

*Then they cried to the Lord in their trouble, and He saved them from their distress.*
Psalm 107:19

Lord, this is my cry for help! The troubles of this world are consuming my thoughts, I call out to You for help. The stress of (name of the struggle) continues to dampen my outlook. I want to change my perspective, I'm shouting out with all I have, please save me from my distress! I believe what You say is true. Your word tells me, You are listening to me right now. I affirm it! You say You love me beyond what my mind could imagine. I accept it! Your word proclaims You heal and reconcile. I declare it! Thank You for hearing **my cry** and moving me to become a person of faith and confidence. I pray this in Jesus name, Amen.

*-Notes-*

_____
_____
_____
_____
_____
_____
_____
_____
_____
_____
_____

# *My Song*

*The LORD is my strength and my shield; my heart trusts in Him, and He helps me. My heart leaps for joy, and with my song, I praise Him.*
Psalm 28:7

Lord, You are my strength. You protect me from my bouts with (name the struggle). I trust You. You help me overcome my sorrowfulness. I've seen your magnificent work in my life and throughout history. You are awe-inspiring. From the inner workings of my soul, all praise and honor I give to You. When I think of Your mighty deeds, I can't help but smile, laugh, shout, and cry out for joy. Though the stresses of my life may not be gone, I know I can endure it all because You are beside me. Thank You for always supporting and protecting me through my difficult times. I will sing **my song** of praise to You now and forever. I pray this in Jesus name, Amen.

*-Notes-*

_____
_____
_____
_____
_____
_____
_____
_____
_____

# *My Conviction*

*For I am convinced that neither death nor life, neither angels nor demons, neither the present nor the future, nor any powers, neither height nor depth, nor anything else in all creation, will be able to separate us from the love of God that is in Christ Jesus our Lord.*
Romans 8:38-39

Lord, though (name the struggle) is stressful, I'm convinced You're with me. Though sometimes I struggle to find a reason to get up in the morning, I'm convinced, You're for me. Though I find myself in dark places at times in my mind, I'm sure You'll lift me up. Though I want to distance myself and isolate, I'm confident You'll draw me closer to You. Though I live in an imperfect and sometimes evil world, I'm persuaded, You'll help me not fall into temptation. Though I feel unloved and there are times when I don't want to love You and others, I am swayed I will never be separated from Your perfect love. This is **my conviction**. Thank You for loving me no matter how much I want to draw from You. I pray this in Jesus name, Amen.

*-Notes-*

_____
_____
_____
_____
_____
_____
_____
_____
_____
_____

# *My Overcomer*

*For everyone born of God overcomes the world. This is the victory that has overcome the world, even our faith. Who is it that overcomes the world? Only the one who believes that Jesus is the Son of God.*
1 John 5:4-5

Lord, I have placed my trust in You for my future. I believe You died on a cross for my sins. You rose from the dead to show me You overcome everything, including death. As I deal with the dirty dishes of life, I will not let them stress me out. I will lean on You for a better attitude. As I endure my difficult seasons, I will not let them drain me. I will rely on Your strength. When a devastating event confronts me, I will not turn to a dark place. I will reach out to You because I know You will pull me out. You are **my overcomer**. Thank You for saving me now from my (name the struggle) and for eternity. I pray this in Jesus name, Amen.

*-Notes-*

_____

_____

_____

_____

_____

_____

_____

_____

_____

# OTHER BOOKS BY DAVID TOWNER

## Today Is My Favorite Day

In 2013, after a series of misfortunes had already fallen on his family, David was diagnosed with cancer. It was during this time that God helped him formulate *six simple truths* about God that would help keep his attitude in check and make each day his favorite. This book is for those who want answers to some of their hardest faith questions. It is a book that will help you confidently say, no matter how dirty the dishes, disappointing the seasons, and devastating the events, *"Today is my favorite day!"*

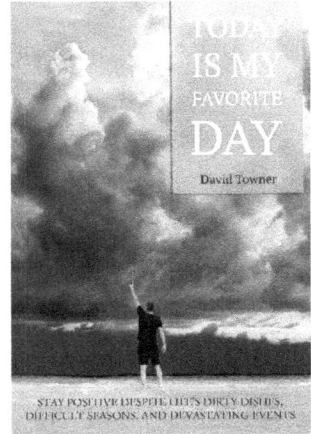

## Today Is My Favorite Day Workbook

David and his wife Tonya co-authored the *Today Is My Favorite Day Workbook* to be used in conjunction with the book to help others delve deeper into the *six simple truths*, develop a more in-depth perspective of God, and experience a new optimistic outlook on life. It is designed to be used individually or with a small group.

61

* 9 7 8 1 7 3 3 3 4 4 2 1 0 *